HISPANIC AMERICA

NEW SPAIN

1600~1760s

BY
ROGER E. HERNÁNDEZ

Marshall Cavendish
Benchmark
New York

Thanks to Stephen Pitti, professor of history and American Studies at Yale University, for his expert reading of this manuscript.

MARSHALL CAVENDISH BENCHMARK
99 WHITE PLAINS ROAD
TARRYTOWN, NEW YORK 10591-5502
www.marshallcavendish.us

LIBRARY OF CONGRESS CATALOGING-IN-PUBLICATION DATA
Hernández, Roger E.
New Spain—1600-1760s / by Roger E. Hernández.
p. cm. — (Hispanic America)
Summary: "Provides comprehensive information on the history of Spanish exploration in the United States"—Provided by publisher.
Includes bibliographical references and index.
ISBN 978-0-7614-2936-4
1. Southwest, New—History—To 1848. 2. Southern States—History—Colonial period, ca. 1600-1775. 3. Spaniards—Southwest, New—History.
4. Spaniards—Southern States—History. I. Title. II. Series.
F799.H45 2009
973.1'6—dc22
2007027215

Photo research by Linda Sykes

Cover photo: The Granger Collection

The photographs in this book are used by permission and through the courtesy of:
The Granger Collection: title page, 4, 7, 22, 32, 42, 63, back cover. Art Resource, NY: Museo Nacional del Virreinato, Tepotzotlan, Mexico/Schalkwijk, 10; Bibliothèque Nationalé, Paris, France/Snark, 24. Houserstock: Baskin Harvey, 12. Courtesy Frederic Remington Art Museum, Ogdensburg, New York: 13. Alamy: Paul Seheult/Eye Ubiquitous, 14, North Wind Picture Archives, 21, 56, 66, 67; The Print Collector, 44; Mary Evans Picture Library, 68. The Bridgeman Art Library: Peter Newark American Pictures, 16, 30. Library of Congress, Washington, DC: 27, 52 ; Florida Museum of Natural History: 28. Courtesy of the Palace of the Governors (MNM/DCA): 35. Corbis: James Amos, 38; Robert Holmes, 39; Bettmann, 41. Mission San Luis: 47. Courtesy Fort King George Historic Site: Photo by Harris Hatcher, 61.

EDITOR: Joy Bean   PUBLISHER: Michelle Bisson
ART DIRECTOR: Anahid Hamparian   SERIES DESIGNER: Kristen Branch

Printed in China
1 3 5 6 4 2

CONTENTS

CHAPTER ONE

SETTLING IN

FOR THE FIRST SEVERAL DECADES AFTER THE famous date of October 12, 1492, when Christopher Columbus first landed in the Western Hemisphere, Europeans in the Americas spent a lot more time looking around than moving in. The discovery of entire unknown continents was so overwhelming to them that, before settling in permanent new homes, they needed to explore the new territories. They were also driven by a thirst for riches like those they found when they conquered Mexico's Aztec Empire.

In order to find new riches, they looked north. In 1513 Juan Ponce de León became the first European to set foot in what is now the United States when he landed in Florida. But he left quickly and was killed when he returned in 1521. Álvar Nuñez Cabeza de Vaca followed him in 1528. His expedition was

Opposite: Columbus discovered the New World when he sailed from Spain and landed in the Americas.

shipwrecked, and for eight years Cabeza de Vaca wandered the Gulf Coast from Florida to Texas, barefoot and nearly naked much of the time, until he ran into other Spaniards, who rescued him. He did not establish settlements either—he was lucky just to survive.

Some twenty years later, two other Spaniards led large, formal expeditions: Hernando de Soto and Francisco Vázquez de Coronado. De Soto explored from Tampa to the Carolinas and west as far as Texas. Coronado concentrated on the southwestern states but also traveled to Kansas. Others spent those years exploring both coasts, reaching Maine on the Atlantic Ocean and Vancouver, Canada, on the Pacific Ocean. None left permanent settlements, even though by the 1550s *conquistadores* were already well established in the Caribbean and also in Mexico and Peru, after conquering the advanced Aztec and Incan civilizations there.

Still, the de Soto and Coronado expeditions helped Spain decide on two locations to start building its empire in North America. One was Florida, a short trip on a sailing ship from the colony in Cuba; the other was the Southwest, an overland trip from the colony in Mexico. Spain hoped the new colonies would bring Indian converts to Christianity, protect against encroachments by the rival empires of England and France, provide gold to enrich the national treasury, and make wealthy men out of the adventurers who set out to settle the two regions.

Florida was first. In 1565 Pedro de Menéndez Avilés

Pedro de Menéndez Avilés (center) landed in Florida and founded Saint Augustine.

founded the city of Saint Augustine. It has endured to this day, and it is the oldest permanent European settlement in what is now the United States. This first Spanish colony predates the first permanent English colony at Jamestown, Virginia, which dates from 1607, and the arrival of the Pilgrims in Plymouth, Massachusetts, in 1620.

The Spanish were the first Europeans to colonize the western side of the country, too. Starting from the day in 1598 that Juan de Oñate crossed the Rio Grande into what is now New Mexico, Spaniards and their American-born descendants (many of them *mestizos* whose ancestors were Spanish and Native American) spread through the West and the Southwest, leaving a cultural legacy that continues to thrive in New Mexico, Arizona, Texas, California, and Colorado.

The Spanish Empire's impact on that region is visible in its architecture, food, peoples, and place names. But the impact is less obvious in Florida—aside from Saint Augustine and a handful of lesser-known sites, the Hispanic influence in Florida is the result of immigration in the relatively recent past, more than a century after the territory became part of the United States in 1821. Still, the region that Spaniards called La Florida (which extended up to the Carolinas) was ruled by Spain for three centuries. It may be an obscure corner of American history, but it is part of American history nonetheless.

SETTLING IN: FLORIDA

Right from the founding of Saint Augustine, everyday life was a struggle for colonists. The soil was sandy in some locations, marshy in others. To plant the maize and squash on which most residents subsisted, men first had to hack away at matted tangles of pine and palmetto roots—and then be satisfied with minimal yields. Homes, churches, and forts were made of local wood and roofed with palm thatch. Buildings quickly rotted in the warm salt air or got knocked down in hurricanes. Everything had to be rebuilt frequently. And no precious metals were found.

Still, the Spaniards persisted. As early as 1566 Menéndez

Avilés established the settlement of Santa Elena on what today is Parris Island, South Carolina. For a short time its population was larger than Saint Augustine's and even supplanted it as the capital of Spanish Florida.

Meanwhile, back in Saint Augustine, the colonists were busy rebuilding yet another fort, their sixth, which they completed in 1586. It did not last long. That same year Sir Francis Drake burned it to the ground along with just about everything else in the settlement. This caused the Spaniards to abandon Santa Elena and to concentrate on Saint Augustine.

American Indians made trouble for the Spaniards, too. In 1597 the Guale tribe killed several Franciscan missionaries. Two years later a fire and a hurricane devastated Saint Augustine. "By the time places like Jamestown, Plymouth, Boston, New York, or Charlestown were founded," wrote historians William S. Coker and Jerrell H. Shofner, "the Spanish settlers in Florida had already experienced raids by Frenchmen and Englishmen, Indian rebellions, severe hurricanes and storms, hunger and thirst, and all of the other problems of a distant and often forgotten frontier colony." As the 1600s began, Spaniards were wondering whether holding on to Florida was worth the trouble. If it did not have gold and silver like Mexico or Peru, why bother?

The Spanish crown decided to keep it because of its strategic value: Saint Augustine could be used as a safe haven for shipwrecked sailors and as a naval base to protect

Spanish shipping from the rival French and English. For this reason, and knowing the colony could not support itself, the Spanish government started to subsidize Saint Augustine with annual payments known as the *situado*, based on the number of military men stationed there. The money came from the treasury in Mexico and was sent to Saint Augustine on treasure ships that sailed out of Havana once a year. By 1580 the Florida colony had three hundred officers and soldiers, which meant it received 65,859 pesos annually.

Florida remained a backwater, never becoming a priority of the Spanish government. Yet the situado and the backbreaking labor of Saint Augustinians were enough, just barely, to keep the colony growing. Coker and Shofner cited a study estimating that the population of European origin increased from 575 in 1641 to 725 in 1671, then to more than 900 in 1701. Another study found that of those coming to Saint Augustine between 1658 and 1691, one out of five were born in Mexico. Yet another study measured *demographics* between 1659 and 1756. Of the white males over that ninety-seven-year period, 38 per-

An oil painting shows the diversity of the people living in Florida.

cent were *peninsulares* born in Spain, approximately 37 percent were native-born *floridianos*, and 16 percent were born elsewhere in Spanish America. Close to 5 percent were foreigners, and 4.5 percent were of African descent, mostly slaves. Of the women, Coker and Shofner said, 85 percent of those found in marriage records were born in Florida.

With its rising *criollo* population, Saint Augustine was developing an identity of its own within the Spanish Empire.

SETTLING IN: NEW MEXICO

A few years later across the North American continent, criollos would begin to create their own identity, too. Unlike Saint Augustine, however, their culture persists to this day.

Spain's colonies in the American Southwest also owe their start to strategic and military concerns. Texas and the Pacific Coast had been explored but not settled by the middle of the 1500s. Then, in 1579, the same Francis Drake who burned down Saint Augustine a few years later plundered Spanish vessels in Pacific waters. The Spanish king decided that the region had to be defended and chose Mexican-born criollo Juan Oñate for the task.

Marching from Mexico with a force "one sixth the size of the force that Menéndez brought to Florida," historian David Weber said in his book *The Spanish Frontier in North America*, Oñate crossed the Rio Grande near present-day El Paso in 1598 and marched through the territory of American Indians the Spaniards came to call Pueblos (*pueblo* is Spanish for vil-

Juan Oñate helped build the first settlement in the southwestern United States.

lage, as these Native Americans lived in towns of multistory dwellings). In present-day New Mexico, Oñate built the Church of San Gabriel, the first European settlement in what is now the southwestern United States, and claimed the land for the king of Spain.

But things did not get off to a good start. Surrounded by hostile Native Americans who remembered Spanish abuses as far back as the Coronado expedition two generations before, and with little support from authorities in Mexico, the colonists came close to giving it all up. "They are as exhausted, hard pressed and in need of help as I am to furnish it," Oñate wrote in 1607, as quoted by historian John L. Kessel in *Spain in the Southwest.* Oñate resigned New Mexico's governorship and was replaced on a temporary basis by Captain Juan Martínez de Montoya.

Martínez de Montoya was rejected by the colonists, who said he was not enough of a military man. So he and a handful of supporters established a separate settlement downriver, which they called Santa Fe. In 1610 the new governor, Pedro de Peralta, officially made it the capital. Santa Fe remains the capital of the state of New Mexico, and it is the second-oldest city in the United States, after

FROM VAQUERO TO COWBOY

The father of the rugged, lone American cowboy is the vaquero of Spanish colonial days. The culture of vaqueros (*vaca* is Spanish for cow) began with the settlers who arrived in New Mexico with their herds in the early 1600s. The first true ranches were set up by the Catholic Church near Mission San Antonio in Texas a century later. Later, after peace with the Apaches, privately owned ranches came to dominate.

Many of today's ranches in South Texas have their origins in that period, predating the American Revolution. Most are not in the hands of descendants of the first owners, yet vaquero traditions survive. The University of Texas "Handbook of Texas Online" says cowboy clothing, equipment, saddle styles, roping methods, and terminology can be traced back to vaquero days.

The elaborate interior of the San Miguel Chapel.

Saint Augustine. Santa Fe's Palace of the Governors and San Miguel Chapel are among the oldest buildings in the country and are classic examples of Spanish colonial architecture.

Like Florida, New Mexico was not a priority for the Spanish crown compared to wealthier colonies in Peru, Mexico, and Cuba. Yet it grew faster than Florida. While Florida's colonists had to travel by ship to arrive or to bring supplies, New Mexico was reachable on horseback, relatively close to the northernmost outposts of the wealthy established colony in Mexico.

How big was the colony in its first years? Kessel estimated that in the 1660s "New Mexico's non-aboriginal population" was about 2,500 people—fewer than the 16,000 in Zacatecas, the chief city of northern Mexico, but more than the few hundred in Saint Augustine. Kessel says that number included peninsulares, criollos, mestizos, and Native Americans "regardless of blood mixture or origin living in a manner more Spanish than Indian, nominally Roman Catholic and Spanish-speaking."

What about *unassimilated* Indians who rejected Catholicism and clung to their ancient ways? In 1638 there were perhaps 40,000 Pueblo inhabitants. Over the next four decades that number declined by half. Some died of diseases that originated in Europe to which they had no immunity. Others became Hispanicized Catholics—they and their mestizo children no longer counted as American Indians in the eyes of Spain.

Whether those conversions were Spain's attempt to save souls for Christianity, or a genocide that destroyed a culture, is an issue still debated today. In New Mexico as well as Florida, Spanish priests played a historical role as influential as that of soldiers and politicians.

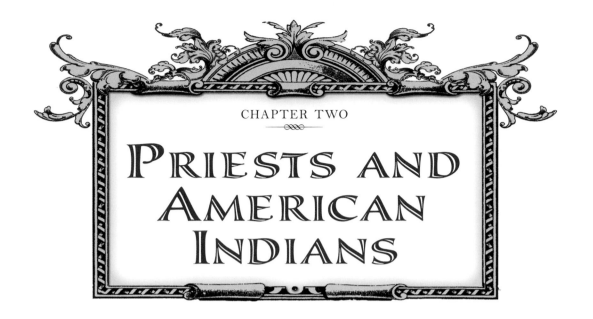

CHAPTER TWO

PRIESTS AND AMERICAN INDIANS

T HROUGHOUT HISTORY, NATIONS HAVE
enacted policies they hoped would make them richer
and more powerful. Sixteenth century Spain, as the
superpower of that era, certainly sought wealth and world
dominance. But it also had another, less worldly ambition.
Spain believed its mission was to convert the uncounted mil-
lions of Native Americans in the newly discovered Americas
to Catholicism.

The goal was supported by the pope himself, who in 1573
declared that "Indians are truly men capable of understanding
the Catholic faith." The Spanish government specifically
called for missionary priests to spread out from the areas
Spain already controlled, such as central Mexico, where many

Opposite: Spanish
missionaries try to
convert Native
Americans to
Catholicism.

American Indians either had already converted to Christianity or had died of disease. The priest were supposed to head toward areas Spain did not yet control, where American Indians still worshipped their old gods. Preaching to natives, said a royal decree of 1537, "is the principal purpose for which we order new discoveries and settlements to be made."

Florida and New Mexico proved especially attractive to missionaries. Both were on the fringes of the Spanish Empire, with more Native Americans yet to be converted and fewer politicians or soldiers to interfere. Members of the Franciscan *religious order* were enthusiastic—in far-off corners of the new continent, they faced less competition from rival orders. Their plan was to move right into Indian communities, with perhaps a small military escort for protection, and convince residents to worship the Christian god. These were the earliest of dozens of Spanish *missions*, small settlements that dotted the southwest (where many survive) and Florida (where most do not). They consisted of a residence or two, perhaps a school to educate American Indian children, and, of course, a church. Priests also introduced American Indians to European life beyond religion. Mission American Indians learned of domestic animals such as cattle, pigs, and chickens; they were trained to use tools such as hammers and saws; and they were taught the Spanish language. American Indians were expected to dress, eat, and act like Spaniards. Priests also destroyed sacred idol statues, ritual masks, and other sacred objects from the their old religions.

In the southwest, the first steps toward bringing Christianity to the Native Americans were taken even before Santa Fe was founded, when a Franciscan named Agustín Rodríguez crossed the Rio Grande in 1581 to establish Spanish contact with the Pueblos—briefly and temporarily—for the first time since the Coronado expedition. Seventeen years later, when Juan Oñate crossed the river to establish the permanent Spanish presence at Santa Fe, Franciscans traveled with him, too.

FIRST MISSIONS

This time, they stayed. A handful of additional priests arrived over the next several years. In a quarter century—with the help of Native-American labor—they built a large number of missions in New Mexico, spread out in the shape of a cross through 200 miles (322 kilometers) of the Rio Grande Valley, in the heart of Pueblo territory. In 1629 a party bringing supplies and a number of new Franciscan priests arrived in Santa Fe after a long

Pueblo communities are spread out through the Rio Grande Valley.

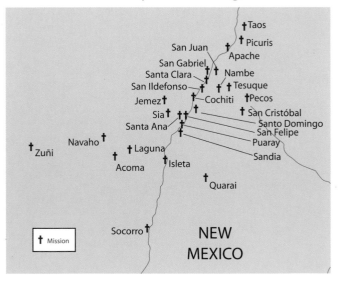

march from Mexico, led by Fray Esteban de Perea, also a Franciscan. The newly arrived priests more than doubled the number of missionaries in the region and quickly established more missions, stretching out to the country of Acoma, Zuni, and Hopi Indians some 250 miles (402 km) away.

A friar named Alonso de Benavides, chief of the Santa Fe missions when Fray Esteban and his fellow priests arrived, later traveled to Spain and wrote of the progress his fellow Franciscans had made. In a report published in 1630, he claimed that 86,000 American Indians had been baptized in New Mexico, among them not only the Pueblo, but also the Navajo and the Apache. Fray Alonso de Benavides insisted that the conversions were voluntary, and that violence was not used as it had been when Coronado had explored the area nearly a century earlier. Instead, he said, divine miracles witnessed by American Indians—for instance, a cross that restored eyesight to a blind boy and holy water that revived a baby—convinced them to convert of their own free will.

Fray Alonso believed the missionaries should expand beyond New Mexico, all the way to the southern Atlantic coast. But preachers had already been at work in that area for decades. When Saint Augustine was founded in 1565, the first priests on the scene were Jesuits. The region the Spanish called Florida included not only the modern state of that name but also Georgia, Alabama, and South Carolina, and the Jesuits stretched it even farther. They built ten missions that reached all the way to Virginia, near

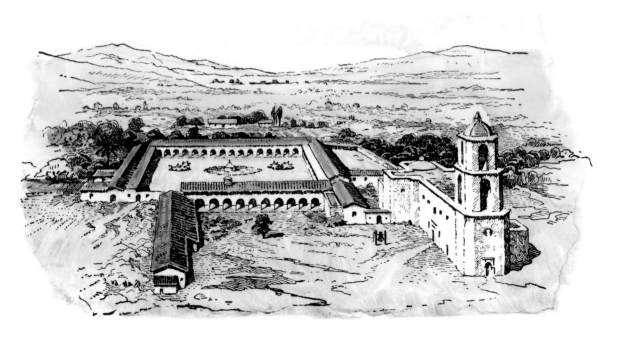

A Spanish colonial mission settlement in North America.

where the English would establish the colony of Jamestown decades later. But American Indian resistance proved so intense that the Jesuits gave up in 1572. A year later Franciscans took their place.

By the early 1600s Franciscans had made progress converting the Timuca Indians around Saint Augustine and the Guales, who lived in southern Georgia. There were setbacks, such as when American Indians killed five friars in an uprising after a native chief was punished for having more than one wife, a custom from the old religion that is prohibited by Christianity. Yet by the 1630s missionaries had reached the Apalachee province, near present-day Tallahassee. Forty years later a string of at least ten missions extended 150 miles (241 km) along the Atlantic Coast north of Saint Augustine, reaching Santa Catalina Island in South Carolina near the border with English-ruled Georgia. To the west there were more than thirty missions, many of them clustered around the Spanish fort San Marco de Apalachee. Overall in Florida, some 70 priests were said to minister to 26,000 native converts.

Even if that figure is an exaggeration, as Weber wrote, there is little doubt that Spanish priests had some success converting American Indians in Florida. Weber also said that the visiting bishop of Cuba (whose territory included Florida) counted some 1,400 residents at Mission San Luis de Talimali, west of Saint Augustine, most of whom were American Indian converts to Catholicism. The bishop also administered the rite of confirmation to 13,152 American Indians. Weber quoted him as saying they "are not idolaters, and they embrace with devotion the mysteries of our holy faith."

Spanish explorer Hernando de Soto (*center, on horse, with sword*) arrives in the United States with his followers.

What no one can know today is how much of that embrace was inspired by true belief, and how much forced by fear. After the Coronado and de Soto expeditions of the 1540s sought to convert Native Americans by violence—leaving tales of Spanish cruelty still remembered when Franciscans returned two generations later—Spanish theologians debated whether it was proper to force unbelievers to become Catholic. After all, some reasoned, if the supposed converts were just pretending, then they had not really converted—and the all-knowing god of Christianity would not be fooled. In 1573 a Spanish royal decree prohibited conversion by violence. The command was not always obeyed in practice, but the more enlightened missionaries in Florida and New Mexico understood the problem. "With suavity and mildness, an obstinate spirit can better be reclaimed than with violence and rigor," wrote Fray Esteban de Perea, the Franciscan who brought in the thirty new priests to boost recruiting efforts in New Mexico.

Yet the same laws that prohibited violence in conversion approved the use of force against American Indians who strayed from their new religion. Those who committed acts of *idolatry* or simply failed to attend mass, Weber said, "were commonly placed in stocks, incarcerated or whipped." In some cases, merely leaving the mission brought corporal punishment. The Native Americans, unsurprisingly, grew resentful.

American Indians employed by the Spanish in a sugar mill.

RESISTANCE

To make matters worse, American Indians were abused in nonreligious matters, too. They were put to labor constructing settlements and they were usually not paid. Weber noted that in 1657 converted American Indians in Florida complained to Governor Diego de Rebolledo that Spanish traders forced them to go along as unpaid porters to the territories of the unconverted. Two years later, Weber wrote, unpaid labor had become such a problem in New Mexico that Governor Bernardo López de Mendizábal issued an edict banning it. But many American Indians quit anyway. They refused to work for the Spaniards even if they got paid.

The New Mexico Indians, as a conquered people, also were required to pay *tribute* to their conquerors the Spaniards, under a system similar to European *feudalism*, known as *encomienda*. Land-owning or high-ranking Spaniards received a royal commission to protect American Indians in exchange for the tribute, which for the typical Pueblo family consisted of cotton cloth payable in the spring and a *fanega* (some three bushels) of maize payable after the autumn harvest. American Indians could also pay in animal hides or other foodstuffs. Those who did not have goods for tribute were forced by encomenderos to pay off their debts with labor; the men would perhaps work in the landowner's farm fields while women became household servants.

In Florida this encomienda system did not take root because settlers never felt strong enough to extract tribute from American Indians on a regular basis. What took its place was *repartimiento*, under which American Indians were sporadically recruited for construction of public works such as bridges and roads. The law required them to labor on these tasks, but it also required they be paid. However, more often than not their Spanish overlords refused to pay them.

Another problem was health. In 1653 smallpox broke out in Florida, and in 1659 measles killed more than 10,000 American Indians. In New Mexico, the drier climate was less conducive to the spread of disease, yet Kessel calculated that smallpox and typhus reduced the number of Pueblo from the 40,000 a priest had reckoned in 1638 to half that number forty years later. These deaths, mostly from diseases unknown before the arrival of Europeans, decimated the populations and threatened the survival of the native cultures.

American Indians started to rebel. Sometimes rebellion took a passive form, with American Indians only pretending to have converted to Christianity while continuing to practice the religion of old or mixing the two religions. While some priests believed idolatry had been banished, the reality was sometimes different. "[M]any natives simply added Jesus, Mary and Christian saints to their rich *pantheons*," Weber wrote.

Up in Arms

When Ponce de León became the first European to set foot in what is now the United States, Florida American Indians met his landing party with a rain of arrows. Explorers who followed him decades later, such as Hernando de Soto and Francisco Vázquez de Coronado, also often fought with American Indians they encountered. These were battles between complete strangers—between Europeans and Native Americans who had never even heard of each other until they spilled the other's blood.

A century later there was still violence, but now it was violence between people who had spent decades getting to know each other: Spanish colonists and neighboring American Indians.

Early in the 1600s violence tended to be localized. In one such case, a priest in New Mexico went out to look for Zunis who were late for mass, but he was stopped by an angry crowd, "smashing his head with their clubs in order to prevent him from preaching the word of God," according to the report from Fray Alonso de Benavides. After killing another priest, the rebels hid in nearby mountains and were chased by Spanish soldiers. An amnesty ended the affair without more bloodshed. Priests went back to preaching; Native Americans grudgingly returned to the pews.

American Indians revolt against the priests trying to convert them and resort to violence.

By the 1670s, though, hostilities were more persistent and more organized. In Florida, what started out as a local incident involving a priest who publicly reprimanded a Chacato chief for having four wives turned into a widespread violent act in which entire villages were wiped out. This time, the offer of amnesty was rejected. Trouble brewed in New Mexico as well. "The whole land is at war with the very numerous nation of the heathen Apache Indians, who kill all the Christian Indians they encounter," said a friar's report. The Spanish New Mexicans mounted retaliatory raids, and a cycle of violence started.

THE FIRST FREE BLACK COMMUNITY

Beginning in the 1670s, as tensions heated up between English Carolinians and Spanish floridianos, enslaved Africans escaped from their English masters to Spanish Florida. Spaniards had slaves of their own. But they figured that welcoming the slaves of their colonial rivals was like taking away their property.

Spanish authorities gave escaped Africans an official sanctuary in 1738. Fort Mose, near Saint Augustine, became home to some one hundred escapees who blended African, Spanish, Native American, and English cultural traditions. It was the first legally recognized settlement of free blacks in the United States. They remained together until 1763, when they, along with most other Saint Augustinans, left for Cuba when Spain ceded Florida to England. Today the site is a National Historic Landmark. A recreation of Fort Mose is seen here.

Pueblo Indians revolt against Spanish invaders in 1680.

Things got worse.

Facing religious bullying, forced labor, failed crops, epidemics, and raids by enemy tribes, Pueblo Indians exploded in anger. A leader named Popé unified many of the 17,000 Pueblo—a people spread out over hundreds of miles and further separated by half a dozen different languages—and on August 9, 1680, led some 2,000 warriors in an attack on Santa Fe. The outpost then had some 1,000 inhabitants but perhaps just 100 Spanish men able to bear arms, wrote Weber. They fought off Popé's men for more than a month. The Pueblos fought hard, too, burning homes and forcing defenders to take cover in an ever-shrinking number of government buildings.

The attackers mocked the Christian faith they believed had been forced upon them. Kessel quoted a report from Governor Antonio de Otermín: "What grieved us most were the dreadful flames from the church and the scoffing and ridicule which the wretched and miserable Indian rebels made of the sacred things." Then the Pueblo cut off Santa Fe's water supply. The Spaniards, with four hundred casualties and no hope of reinforcement, fled Santa Fe on September 21. They marched through 300 miles (483 km) of dangerous Apache territory and took refuge across the Rio Grande south of El Paso, on the Mexican side of today's border.

Native Americans and colonists alike understood this was no mere flare-up like the clashes of the past. This time the American Indians had mounted the first organized large-scale rebellion in the Spanish Southwest and had forced colonists to abandon the settlement they had built in what is now the United States.

In Florida, Spaniards also found themselves on the retreat. American Indians in this region never did manage a rebellion as widespread and powerful as Popé's, but they did find anti-Spanish allies in the British settlers colonizing the Carolinas. The same year that Santa Fe fell, a force of British Carolinians and American Indian allies attacked the northernmost Spanish missions on Jekyll and Saint Catherine's Islands, in the province of Guale. Spain abandoned the settlements. There were also attacks on missions to the west of Saint Augustine, near present-day Tallahassee.

By the 1690s, with most of New Mexico and northern Florida abandoned, the Spanish Empire in what would become the United States was barely hanging on. It looked like it was going to come apart. Now it was facing not only American Indian rebels, but also a serious challenge from British and French rivals for colonial supremacy.

CHAPTER THREE

SETTLED IN

D ESPITE ITS PRECARIOUS SITUATION AS THE seventeenth century turned into the eighteenth, Spain stayed in North America for more than a hundred years longer. The colonists lost some regions, regained control of others, and asserted themselves politically, economically, and culturally where they could.

Even before Spain regained control of Santa Fe, priests began to explore present-day Arizona and California. Foremost among them was Eusebio Francisco Kino, a Jesuit who in 1687 arrived in the region then called Pimería Alta, which included the northern part of the Mexican state of Sonora and southern Arizona. Kino brought the mission system to the region, beginning with the founding of Nuestra Señora

Opposite: American Indians welcome explorers to California.

de los Dolores the year he arrived. From then until 1692 he established some twenty missions and earned a reputation for treating American Indians with kindness. Father Kino also has gone down in history as an explorer and maker of maps. After travels that covered some 50,000 square miles in the region, he drew the first known maps of Pimería Alta and Baja California.

While the Jesuit was exploring Arizona, other Spaniards were planning to take Santa Fe back from the Pueblo. Many spent the period in El Paso—which was then located in the present-day Mexican city of Juárez—in poverty and frustration at their inability to return to Santa Fe. They also faced more revolts from American Indians who lived just below today's United States-Mexico border.

Meanwhile, dissent tore apart the unity of Pueblo who held Santa Fe. Popé, after setting himself up in the Governor's Palace that the Spaniards had left behind, visited American Indian communities followed by a large armed force to demand that his fellow Pueblo give up Christianity and return to the old religion. Popé destroyed crosses and Catholic saint statues, ordering that "anyone who might still keep in his heart a regard for the priests, the governor and the Spaniards . . . would be punished." He became to many Native Americans just as tyrannical as the Spanish priests who also punished people because of their religious beliefs. These quarrels among the Pueblo weakened them, opening the road for Spaniards to return.

THE RECONQUEST OF SANTA FE

The man who led them back was Diego de Vargas, who in 1691 arrived in El Paso. He had been appointed governor of New Mexico, but that meant little—the province was controlled by American Indians. Vargas set out to change that. He learned of the Pueblo infighting caused by Popé's abuses and convinced many American Indians to switch sides. In 1693 he felt strong enough to take Santa Fe with an army of eight hundred Spaniards and Native-American allies. With prayers to an image of the Virgin Mary, Nuestra Señora de la Conquista (still venerated by New Mexican Hispanics), he chased the Pueblo out of Santa Fe and the nearby lands. It had taken thirteen years for Hispanic New Mexicans to fully reestablish themselves in Santa Fe. Three years later another Pueblo rebellion broke out, but Vargas's men squashed it quickly.

The Spanish New Mexicans were again in control. And the uprisings had come to the

Diego de Vargas led his army to take over Santa Fe.

Pueblo at a high cost—Weber estimated their population sank from 17,000 when Santa Fe fell to 14,000 in 1700. Battle deaths accounted for most of the decline.

There were changes when Spain returned. Not wishing to incite another revolt, priests became less strict, allowing the Pueblo to mix some of their old ceremonies with Catholic rituals. Forced-labor requirements also eased up, as the encomienda system was never restored. American Indians felt less like serfs and freer to come and go and select the kind of work they preferred. The Spanish government also tried to encourage more artisans and tradesmen to settle in Santa Fe. In a recruiting mission to Mexico City, home of the *viceroyalty*, three Santa Fe residents convinced some sixty families to leave their homes and start new lives on the edge of New Spain. "The men's occupations varied," Kessel wrote. "Barber, blacksmith, cabinetmaker, cartwright, chandler, filigree maker, coppersmith, cutler, miller, mining amalgamator, musician, painter, paver, stone and brick mason, and weaver." These families intermarried, which provided a social stability Santa Fe had never known.

FLORIDA ON THE BRINK

Historians have not found evidence of much communication or travel between Santa Fe and Saint Augustine, some 1,700 miles. Spanish Florida's capital never fell to American Indians, like its southwestern counterpart. Yet out in the fringes of Spanish Florida—itself a fringe region of the empire—Spain began to lose ground it had gained at the peak of its mission system in the 1670s. In large part this was due to competition from Great Britain. After losing Guale to the British and their American Indian allies in 1680, Spain found itself on the defensive. British Carolinians and American Indian allies devastated missions to the west of Saint Augustine, selling Hispanicized Indians into slavery. Spain held on to little more than the fortress settlements of Saint Augustine, Pensacola, and San Marcos de Apalachee. All three were minor settlements compared to Spain's riches in Mexico City, Lima, and Havana. Even Saint Augustine, Spanish Florida's capital, was a backwater. Jonathan Dickinson, an Englishman who visited in 1696 during a period of peace between Spain and Britain, wrote in his diary that Saint Augustine was just three-quarters of a mile long and had only three hundred able-bodied men to guard it. He seemed more impressed, however, by "a large fortification . . . about thirty feet high, built of sawed stone, such as they get out of the sand between the sea and the sound." He added that the Spanish authorities "would not admit us to come near the fort."

Dickinson might have been the first Britishman to see Castillo de San Marcos, a newly built fortress that in years to come allowed Saint Augustine to stay in Spanish hands. The building still stands today, the oldest fort in the United States.

The difference between San Marcos and the forts that preceded it was that colonists finally stopped using wood, which quickly rotted in the humid air or was destroyed in

An aerial view of Castillo de San Marcos.

hurricanes. The new material was a type of stone called *coquina*, which consisted of crushed seashells quarried from Anastasia Island across the bay from mainland Saint Augustine. A Cuban-born military engineer named Ignacio Daza designed the structure, and stone masons from Havana cut the heavy blocks of coquina for the fortresses' walls. Construction began in 1672 but was often interrupted because of financial woes and was not completed until 1695. Over the next decades it would allow the Spanish of Saint Augustine to turn back two attacks by the powerful British navy.

Those decades marked a turning point in the history of

SPANISH SYNAGOGUE

Spain's northernmost frontier in North America never reached New York City. Yet there was a Spanish settlement there, of sorts, when it was controlled by the Netherlands and called New Amsterdam. The settlement was Shearith Israel Synagogue, founded in 1654 by twenty-three Dutch Jews of Spanish and Portuguese descent whose ancestors fled the Iberian Peninsula to escape religious persecution. When Britain conquered the city in 1664, Shearith Israel continued to thrive. It was the only Jewish congregation in the city until 1825. The synagogue still stands today in New York city.

Spanish North America. In Florida, and a little later in New Mexico, too, the struggle was transformed. No longer was it primarily a fight between Spanish colonists and Native Americans. Beginning in the 1700s, it became one battleground in a war for global dominance among the great powers of Spain, Great Britain, and France.

FIRST SKIRMISHES OF A FUTURE WAR

Containing the British and the French was one reason Spain had decided to settle New Mexico and Florida. But for the first few decades, hard living conditions and American Indian uprisings distracted Spanish colonial officials from that goal. As late as 1630, authorities disregarded Fray Alonso Benavides's recommendation to bring Irish priests who knew the English language to New Mexico to combat British influence. The British were only remembered when they attacked.

But as the century wore on, battles became so frequent that the British and the French replaced American Indians as a principal threat to the Spanish. While Great Britain was destroying Spain's outposts beyond Saint Augustine and Apalachee, France began to assert itself on the Gulf Coast, which Spain claimed for itself, and France's encroachment threatened Spain's southwestern settlements.

The first attempt was led by René Robert Cavalier, Sieur de La Salle, who started a colony at the mouth of the Mississippi River in 1685. Spaniards had forgotten about the region since de Soto and other explorers had visited it more than a century earlier. But when they learned that the French had established a foothold, Carlos II's Council of War decided to "remove this thorn which has been thrust into the heart of America." But it took the Spaniards eleven expeditions over four years to find La Salle's fort. When they found it in 1689, it was in ruins. Alonso de León, who led the expedition, reported he "found all the houses sacked, all the chests, bottle-cases

and all the rest of the settlers' furniture broken." There were just two surviving Frenchmen, living with Indians. They told León that La Salle had been killed by his own men, and that nearly everybody else had died of disease, hunger, and American Indian arrows.

René Robert Cavalier, Sieur de La Salle, claims the Mississippi valley for France.

The first French attempt to take over territory that Spain claimed as its own had failed. Nevertheless, Spain tried to forestall further French encroachments. The first move was to expand into what today is the state of Texas. When searching for La Salle, León had contacted friendly Caddos Indians, who had told him they were interested in Christianity. In 1690 he returned with priests and soldiers and established San Francisco de los Tejas in east Texas. But local tribes that had once been welcoming rebelled three years later and chased the Spanish out, the same year colonists retook Santa Fe. Spain left Texas for twenty years.

Still, the French threat was not forgotten in the 1690s. The key, Spain decided, was to prevent rival powers from controlling the gulf. In the late 1680s Spanish explorers rediscovered Pensacola Bay, which Tristan de Luna had enthusiastically described a century earlier. They pressed Carlos II to authorize and fund an expedition to build a base in Pensacola, but the king was indecisive. It took several reports of French and English incursions into the region for him to finally agree. In 1698 Spain began construction of a fort in Pensacola. For more than a century to follow, it was the leading settlement in Spanish Florida outside of Saint Augustine.

But it was not enough to stop colonial rivals. Just one year after the Spanish built their fort at Pensacola, a

Pierre LeMoyne, Sieur d'Iberville, was responsible for building Fort Maurepas.

French force under Pierre LeMoyne, Sieur d'Iberville, sailed into a channel that turned out to be an entryway into the Mississippi River, near the present-day town of Biloxi. D'Iberville built Fort Maurepas and sailed to France for reinforcements. He knew the significance of the discovery. For one thing, France could now control the mouth of a river "highway" that could take French traders and colonists deep into the heart of the North American continent. Also, the discovery split Spanish Florida from the Spanish Southwest.

A new century was dawning then, and with it came major changes in the international balance of power—in relations among Great Britain, France, and Spain—that profoundly affected the North American empires of those three nations. What set things off was the death of Spain's king, Carlos II. Although he was a member of the Spanish-Austrian Hapsburg dynasty, which opposed the French Bourbon dynasty, the childless king shocked all of Europe when he named Phillipe d'Anjou, the grandson of France's Bourbon King Louis XIV, as his heir.

Worried that if France and Spain united under the Bourbons they would become too powerful, Britain, Austria, and other powers went to war seeking to over throw Felipe V from the Spanish throne. Echoes of what historians call the War of the Spanish Succession would be heard in New Mexico and Florida.

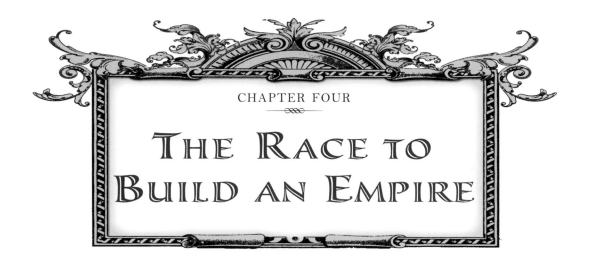

CHAPTER FOUR

THE RACE TO BUILD AN EMPIRE

RELATIONS BETWEEN FRANCE AND SPAIN improved after Phillipe d'Anjou became the new Spanish king, Felipe V. After all, the two nations were now ruled by a grandfather and his grandson, members of the royal house of Bourbon. So even though there had been centuries of war and mistrust between them, Spain allowed France to get on with its new colony of Louisiana, right in the middle of the North American continent and separating Spanish Florida from Spanish New Mexico.

France spread up the Mississippi River Valley and even moved its outpost in Biloxi to Mobile, Alabama, territory claimed by the Spanish as part of its Florida province even though it was not occupied by them. Against the advice of his ministers, Felipe V did not protest his grandfather's expansion. The French went

Opposite: Louis XIV proclaims duc d'Anjou king of Spain.

north as far as Detroit, which they founded in 1701, and to the outskirts of Spanish Pensacola. The influence the French gained among American Indians there worried the Spanish, but they still kept the peace with their uneasy new ally.

The Bourbon family connection was not the only reason for the apparent friendliness. Spain and France also needed each other to fight the British. Back in Europe, the War of Spanish Succession raged as armies fought each other across the continent in large set-piece battles involving tens of thousands of soldiers.

ATTACK ON FLORIDA

In one of the first encounters, a force of British soldiers and American Indian allies under Carolina governor James Moore charged into Spanish Florida and wreaked widespread havoc. The invasion came from land and sea, centering first on Saint Augustine. Moore's troops burned down Saint Augustine, as the British had under Sir Francis Drake a century earlier. But this time Moore could not claim a victory, because most of the approximately 1,200 Saint Augustinians found refuge inside the formidable Castillo de San Marcos. Moore bombarded it, but the fortress's massive coquina walls withstood the siege, and the Spanish stashed supplies for the entire populace. They held on for two months, until a Spanish fleet from Havana appeared on the horizon. Moore did not want to get caught in a trap, so he burned his ships and retreated by land back to Carolina.

After his failure to take San Marcos, Moore was forced to resign the governorship. But it was not the last Spanish Florida would hear from him. In 1704, Moore raised a private army of 1,500 Indians that destroyed most of the Apalachee missions, subjecting their inhabitants—Native American and Spanish alike—to torture. One report had it that the out-of-control soldiers took a Spaniard and "slashed him all over, stuck burning splinters in the wounds and set fire to him." Moore boasted he had killed or enslaved 325 men and 4,000 women and children, Weber said.

By late 1706, additional raids had destroyed most of what was left of the approximately forty Spanish missions that dotted Florida. Within two years, as Spain's colonial

The mission at San Luis de Apalachee was mostly destroyed in the 1700s, but this chapel was rebuilt on the site.

governor reported, the British had taken perhaps 10,000 American Indians to Carolina as slaves. Ironically, historians have said that Moore's success was due in part to his ability to win over American Indian allies, who fought the Spanish and helped the British capture enemy American Indians to be made slaves. Native American hated the Spaniards for forcing them into hard labor at little pay away from their homes, while the British "offered powerful incentives in the form of rum, arms, ammunition, booty and cheap trade goods." The ploy was effective. Unlike reconquered Santa Fe, interior Florida never went back to full Spanish control. Only Saint Augustine and Pensacola stayed relatively safe in Spanish hands, along with neighboring villages. Everywhere else was American Indian territory, Spanish in name only.

At least, Spain must have thought, the British did not control Florida, either. An attack on Pensacola failed in 1711, leaving the fort under the Spanish. Officials from there and from Saint Augustine asked for the help of French forces in Louisiana; one report from a Spanish officer says Pensacola would have been abandoned were it not for French aid. This Franco-Spanish alliance was not merely defensive. A combined force marched from Saint Augustine north and laid siege to Charleston. But the British resisted, and the invading soldiers turned around and went home.

The War of Spanish Succession ended in 1714. At first glance, it seemed like a draw. In Europe, Felipe V remained king of Spain but signed a treaty removing himself as heir to the throne of France. In North America, Spain kept its southwestern colonies and Florida; France held on to Louisiana; and Great Britain stayed in Carolina and points north to New England. But in reality, Spain was weakened by the loss of its string of missions across Florida.

SPAIN IN TEXAS

In the southwest, however, the impact of the war was not as strong. British colonies were too far away to mount much of an offensive. In fact, while it was losing ground in Florida during the first decade and a half of the 1700s, Spain not only reconquered Santa Fe, but also began to build missions beyond New Mexico and Father Kino's Pimería Alta. The Spanish first went into Texas, and years later they entered California.

The Spanish thrust into Texas came about because of the fear the French would make a thrust of their own. The French had indeed been trying to make inroads into Texas since at least the 1690s, when Spanish officials heard American Indian tales of other white men in the region. What is more, French firearms had been found in the hands of Apaches. At least one French expedition, in 1703, left Louisiana to explore New Mexico for gold. But by the early 1700s Spain and France had become allies in the war against Great Britain. They were too busy fighting to pay attention to forgotten, uncolonized Texas.

That began to change with the end of the War of Spanish

Succession. When the fighting was over, relations between France and Spain became tense. The latter closed its ports to French traders. But France began once again to covet the Spanish Southwest. Spain reacted by returning to Texas for the first time since Alonso de León evacuated it in 1690.

The return took a roundabout path. The year the war ended, French Louisiana's governor Antoine de la Mothe, Sieur de Cadillac, received a letter from Francisco Hidalgo, a Spanish priest who had been in Texas during the previous Spanish attempt to colonize it. Father Francisco said that when the Spaniards left he had told the Caddos tribes that he would return, but other Spanish officials had shown no interest. Without actually saying so, he was telling the French that Texas was wide open. But was it all a ploy? Weber wrote that Hidalgo had

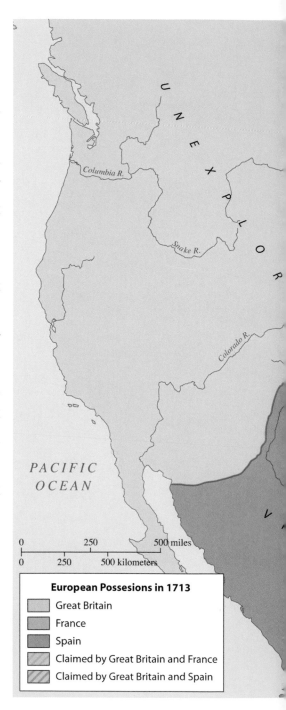

PACIFIC
OCEAN

0   250   500 miles
0   250   500 kilometers

European Possesions in 1713
Great Britain
France
Spain
Claimed by Great Britain and France
Claimed by Great Britain and Spain

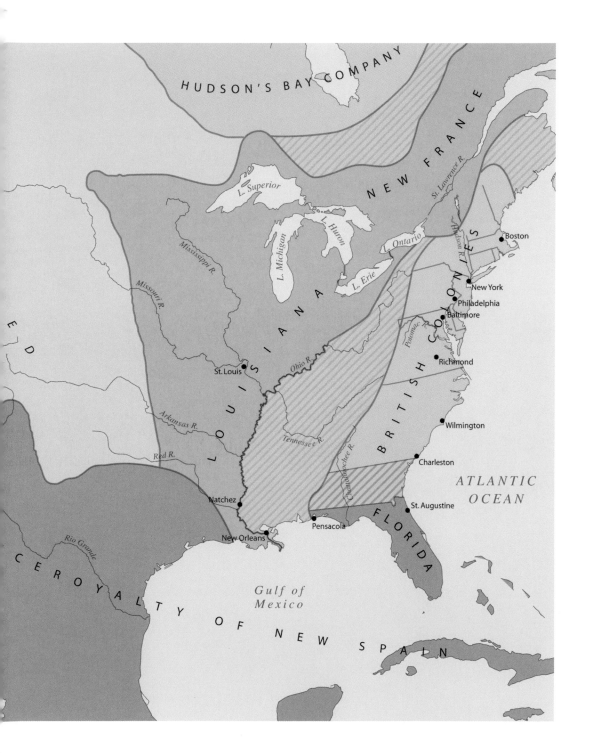

HUDSON'S BAY COMPANY

NEW FRANCE

L. Superior

Mississippi R.

L. Michigan

L. Huron

St. Lawrence R.

Ontario

L. Erie

Hudson R.

● Boston

● New York

● Philadelphia

● Baltimore

Missouri R.

L O U I S I A N A

Ohio R.

Potomac R.

B R I T I S H   C O L O N I E S

St. Louis ●

● Richmond

Arkansas R.

Tennessee R.

Chattahoochee R.

● Wilmington

Red R.

● Charleston

ATLANTIC
OCEAN

Natchez ●

St. Augustine ●

F L O R I D A

Rio Grande

Pensacola ●

New Orleans ●

C E R O Y A L T Y   O F   N E W   S P A I N

*Gulf of
Mexico*

E D

THE RACE TO BUILD AN EMPIRE

"apparently invited French officials to send missionaries into Texas, calculating their presence would provoke a Spanish counter response."

Ploy or not, that was how it worked out. In 1714 Cadillac sent a small band of explorers who made their way to the Spanish frontier fortress at San Juan Bautista. The captain in charge there, Diego Ramón, became alarmed, fearing that the handful of Frenchmen was the advanced guard of a larger force. "If His Majesty does not intervene, the French will be masters of all this land," he said. The viceroy in Mexico City then ordered the reoccupation of Texas to stop the French. Ramón moved quickly and established two missions in East Texas, west of a French settlement at Natchitoches.

In a way, it was a show of weakness. By building missions on the other side of the Red River from the French settlements instead of attacking, Spain was unofficially acknowledging that Louisiana belonged to France. But in another way it was a show of strength: Spain had drawn a line in the sand that it would not allow France to cross.

And France never did. More Spaniards poured in. In 1716 the viceroy in Mexico City appointed a Texas governor for the first time—Martín de Alarcón. Two years later he made a lasting contribution. Alarcón was ordered to build a way station halfway between New Mexico and the new East Texas missions. In the oak-covered hills there, Alarcón founded a villa, or country estate, called Béjar, and a mission named for the viceroy, Antonio de Valero. Béjar

The Spanish
mission of the
Alamo.

developed into today's city of San Antonio. The mission later became known as the Alamo—the site of a fierce battle more than a century later between Mexican troops (Mexico controlled the area after gaining independence from Spain) and Texans who sought to break from Mexico and establish their own independent republic.

AT WAR AGAIN

In 1718, the Spanish founded San Antonio, they also reestablished their old fortress in Apalachee, making their position stronger both in Florida and in the southwest. France also made itself stronger that year with the founding of New Orleans, which would become France's largest city in the region. The following year, a new conflict broke out in Europe—the War of the Quadruple Alliance. France, Great Britain, Holland, and Austria were on one side, while Spain fought alone on the other. The war started because the four allies were worried Spain was gaining too much power in Italy. But fighting spread across the Atlantic. Now Spain could not count on French help against Great Britain—it had to fight both.

Actually, this time the British were not much of a threat because American Indian raids had weakened the colony at Carolina. Settlers there had no thought of attacking Saint Augustine, as they had in the past. Instead, they feared a Spanish invasion. But it never came because the Spanish were busy fighting the French. A force of about one hundred men who set out to look for Frenchmen in New Mexico were massacred by American Indians instead. French troops conquered the new Spanish settlements in East Texas, and in Florida, Pensacola fell to a French siege. In response Spain organized the largest fighting force it ever sent into Texas, some five hundred men whose mission went beyond merely taking back East Texas. King Felipe V also wanted them to throw France out of Louisiana, which the Spanish still insisted legally belonged to them.

But the end of the war in Europe ended the expedition. France and Spain became allies once again. Pensacola went back to Spain, and the French force in East Texas withdrew to French territory. King Felipe V called off the invasion of Louisiana. The three powers remained in North America no weaker and no stronger than before the war, except that it was now clear to Spain that the British and the French were not temporary interlopers. They would not be driven out of the territory Spain claimed for itself.

CHAPTER FIVE

HOLDING ON

NORTH AMERICA'S EUROPEAN COLONIAL powers spent the decades after the War of the Quadruple Alliance pushing and elbowing one another, each trying to make more room for itself at the expense of the other. They kept a wary eye on American Indians, too, sometimes forming alliances, sometimes fighting them. They all fought more or less to a standstill—until the American Revolution gave rise to a new power that changed everything. But the emergence of the United States was still almost three-quarters of a century away.

One element that did make Spain weaker than her rivals was trade. For one thing, Spain was no longer the economic powerhouse it had been in the 1500s—it was now poorer than England and France. Also, the North American holdings of both

Opposite: Florida's Saint Augustine was still under Spanish control in the 1700s.

France and Great Britain were the jewels in the crowns of their empires; in contrast, Florida and the southwest remained unimportant backwaters to Spain. Spain thought these areas would lose them money, but they were necessary outposts to protect the richer and much more populous colonies in Mexico, the Caribbean, and South America. Floridianos felt unwanted, and to get the goods they resorted to smuggling along borders with their colonial rival.

APACHE V. COMANCHE V. SPANIARDS

In Texas, Spanish settlements expanded in the first decades of the 1700s. Less than ten years after the founding of San Antonio, Spanish Texas had grown to ten missions and four *presidios*. But there were only 268 soldiers and a total Hispanic population of 400 to 500 people. Part of the problem was that after the wars against the French and British, Spain's Native-American enemies had acquired firearms and had learned to ride horses, which had made them much more effective fighters.

The Apache, for instance, regularly raided San Antonio in the 1720s and 1730s. But the settlement survived—the Apache were more interested in stealing horses and cattle than in conquest. They had been pushed south into Texas and New Mexico by their enemies, the Comanche. Eventually they too entered Spanish territory—with more than just horse-rustling in mind. In 1758 some 2,000 Comanche and allies destroyed a mission the Spanish had recently built at San Sabá, to the west of San Antonio. "They were adorned with the pelts and tails of wild beasts," one priest later wrote about the attacking Indians. Significantly, however, the priest noted that one chief was "ceremonially dressed in vestments of war, with a red coat from a French uniform." Colonists mounted a punitive expedition and found the Comanche armed with French muskets entrenched in a fortified, European-style stockade flying a French flag. The Spanish commander, seeing the Comanche strength and not trusting the Apache allies who made up most of his troops, decided not to mount an attack.

The Spanish would never really control Texas west of San Antonio. But they held on to their grip on the eastern end. There, on the Franco-Spanish frontier, things were peaceful even though Frenchmen armed the Comanche, and the Spanish never gave up their claim that Louisiana legally belonged to them. Colonists on either side of the border traded with each other and even intermarried—in 1736, for instance, the daughter of the captain of Spain's Los Adaes presidio married a French soldier from the neighboring settlement of Natchitoches. Things quieted on the Apache front, too. In 1749 they agreed to peace with the mission at San Antonio, "literally burying a hatchet as well as a lance, six arrows and a live horse in the plaza," Weber wrote. The agreement permitted San Antonio to grow in relative peace.

All across the Spanish Southwest there were attempts to

increase the Hispanic population. Officials offered free transportation, land, and supplies to peasants willing to make the journey across the ocean, but only about fifty people from the Canary Islands settled in San Antonio, bringing the Hispanic population of Texas to about five hundred in 1731. By the 1760s the Hispanic population of the province had doubled. The figure does not include El Paso, which was then part of New Mexico. There, the non-American Indian population was 9,580. The largest city was El Paso, followed by Santa Fe.

JENKIN'S EAR

Nearly 2,000 miles (3,219 km) away in Spanish Florida, the population remained stagnant while the number of rival British settlers to the north grew at a rapid pace. One study estimates that in 1745, 20,300 British colonists lived in Carolina, compared to only 2,100 Spanish colonists living in Florida. The edge in population gave the British confidence to push into Spanish territory.

The 1720s and 1730s were marked by British attempts to expand their dominions further south. The two nations nearly went to war in 1721 when the British built Fort King George in the present-day state of Georgia, territory the British had recognized as Spanish since they signed a treaty in 1670. The following year British settlers and American Indian allies destroyed a village of Yamasee Indians, allies of the Spanish who lived on the outskirts of Saint Augustine.

And in 1733, Great Britain established the colony of Georgia, officially taking over the region that at least in name had been Spain's. It was not long before Georgia governor James Oglethorpe built Fort George, just 50 miles (80.4 km) north of Saint Augustine. It was located in the same Guale area Spain had evacuated in 1680 under British pressure, and it cut off the road to the Spanish fort at Apalachee.

Spain built new forts in the area to counter the British move, but did not have enough troops to garrison them effectively until reinforcements arrived from Cuba in the late 1730s. By then another European war spilled over into colonial North America.

Fort King George still stands in present-day Georgia

It was called the War of Jenkins' Ear because it was sparked by British navy captain named Robert Jenkins, when they said his ear had been cut off by Spanish sailors when they boarded his ship. The first move was made by Oglethorpe, whose troops took the small Spanish posts between Georgia and Saint Augustine. In 1740 he laid siege to Saint Augustine itself, as his predecessor James Moore had in 1702. Just as had happened back then, colonists from the settlements surrounding Saint Augustine took refuge inside Castillo de San Marcos. Once again the fortress's thick coquina walls withstood British cannonades. Oglethorpe withdrew. Two years later the Spanish invaded Georgia with a force of 2,000 men and overcame several small British forts. But the British prevailed at the Battle of Bloody Marsh on Saint Simons Island. It was Spain's last significant challenge to British rule in Georgia.

The war dragged on with minor raids and counterattacks until 1748. No land changed hands with the peace treaty, yet Spanish Florida emerged weakened. Lands beyond Saint Augustine, Pensacola, and Apalachee remained unsettled; few newcomers arrived in those three towns that Spain did control; and the British population continued to outpace the Spanish even after Canary Islanders were persuaded to move to Saint Augustine in 1750. By the start of the next decade the 3,000 Hispanics living in Florida were vastly outnumbered by 6,000 British in Georgia and 38,600 British in South Carolina. While commerce and industry

thrived in the British colonies, Spanish Florida remained little more than three isolated military garrisons.

British Georgia governor James Oglethorpe is shown (center) in this wood engraving with colonists at Savannah, Georgia.

CALIFORNIA, HERE THEY COME

California was the last of the regions in the American West to be settled by Spain. Its coast had been explored by Juan Rodríguez Cabrillo in the 1540s and Sebastián Vizcaíno in the early 1600s, but they established no settlements. The Baja California peninsula in Mexico was colonized, however, and from there the Spanish eventually spread north and built missions in Alta California, the old name for today's state of California.

Spain started these missions to stop Russia from expanding its own empire along the Pacific Coast. Baja California governor José de Gálvez named Captain Gaspar de Portolá to command the first expedition and put Father Junípero Serra in charge of religious issues. The two men moved quickly. In July 1769 Portolá's expedition marched from Baja California to San Diego Bay, where they met sailors from a ship Portolá had sent days earlier and established the first European A settlement in California. From there he and some sixty followers moved north "to break a new trail along a coast known to Spaniards only from the sea," as Weber wrote, fighting rugged terrain and even surviving earthquakes. By October they had established outposts in present-day Los Angeles, Santa Barbara, and San Francisco.

Father Serra founding Mission San Diego in July 1769.

A few days after Portolá left San Diego, Father Serra founded Mission San Diego de Alcalá, California's first. At first, he wrote, American Indians "treated us with as much confidence and goodwill as if they had known us all their lives." Eventually relations soured, as they did everywhere Europeans and Native Americans came into contact. Yet the mission system expanded, especially after explorers in the mid-1770s established supply routes to Baja. Nine missions were founded in Alta California between 1769 and 1784, when Father Serra died. Eventually there would be twenty-one. They have been restored as reminders of a Spanish age long ago.

WAR AGAIN: LANDS CHANGE HANDS

The years just before the founding of California's first mission were of dramatic importance in North America, not just for Spain but also for the other colonial powers, Great Britain and France. In Europe yet another *dynastic* struggle was being fought, this time over succession to the Austrian throne, which eventually expanded into a war that included nearly every nation in Europe. Combatants faced off not only in Europe itself, but also in Asia, Canada, and even Pennsylvania and New York State. Americans know the conflict as the French and Indian War.

The Spanish holdings in North America remained fairly peaceful. But in Cuba a powerful British fleet overtook Havana's defenders in 1762 and occupied the city until a peace treaty ended hostilities one year later. It was this peace treaty that turned upside down the carefully constructed empires that Spain, France, and Great Britain had painstakingly built for nearly two hundred years in what is now the United States.

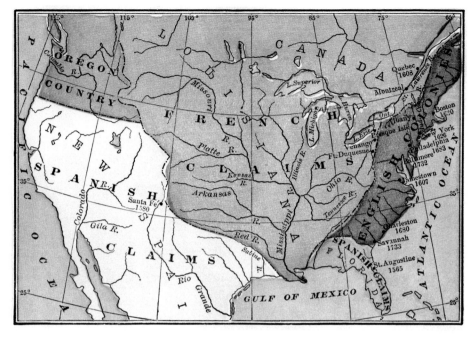

North American British, Spanish, and French colonies before the French and Indian War.

In exchange for giving Havana back to Spain, Great Britain was awarded Spanish Florida. And perhaps as a reward to Spain for entering the war on the side of France, France ceded its Louisiana territory west of the Mississippi to Spain. The remainder of French Louisiana, east of the Mississippi, went to Great Britain.

So even though the entire southwest—Texas, New Mexico, Arizona, and California—remained under Spanish control (a claim American Indians continued to challenge), everything east of that and south of Great Britain's thirteen colonies changed masters. Local people were shocked when they heard news of what kings and ministers had decided across the ocean in Europe. "Spanish officials who had

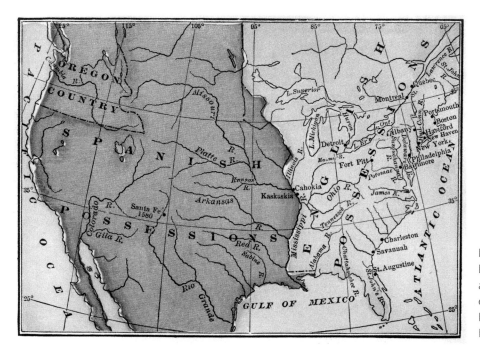

North American British, Spanish, and French colonies after the French and Indian war.

labored long but unsuccessfully to check the growth of Spanish influence from Louisiana learned that the French province had passed suddenly into Spanish hands. Conversely, Spaniards who had successfully defended Pensacola, San Marcos de Apalachee, and St. Augustine against Indians and foreigners discovered that their king had surrendered Florida to Britain without a fight," Weber wrote.

In Florida nearly every Spanish colonist left when the British took over. Some 3,000 men, women, and children (including 83 American Indians and 350 black slaves) moved from Saint Augustine to Havana. In Pensacola all but one of the approximately seven hundred inhabitants sailed to Veracruz, Mexico. Rid of Spanish settlers, the British poured in.

A portrait of King Carlos III.

In contrast, most French colonists stayed put when Spain took over Louisiana. The policy of Carlos III—regarded by historians as the best Spanish Bourbon king until the present era—was to leave the French governing structure as unchanged as possible. So the new governor, Antonio de Ulloa, let his French counterpart stay in office to rule jointly, kept the French flag flying, and brought French troops into the Spanish army. French and Spanish residents got along for a while, but eventually Spain's restrictive trading system (Ulloa ended commerce between Louisiana and France) made merchants angry. They revolted in 1768 and chased Ulloa to Havana, which left the province without a governing authority until 2,000 Spanish troops returned the following year to restore order. This time the new governor, a Spaniard of Irish ancestry named Alejandro O'Reilly, reversed the previous policies and imposed direct Spanish rule.

AMERICANS ON THE HORIZON

Still, the province remained French in culture and language. Even the 2,000 Andalusians and Canary Islanders who arrived in the 1770s were not enough to Hispanicize Louisiana. The 5,700 Frenchmen who stayed when Ulloa arrived remained the majority population.

Florida, however, became Spanish again after twenty years of British rule. During the American Revolution, Spanish troops under Bernardo de Gálvez (a nephew of the Baja California governor) ousted British forces from their outposts on the Mississippi and from Mobile and Pensacola, taking West Florida back for Spain. When the war ended with the Treaty of Paris in 1783, Britain also returned East Florida to Spanish hands and its capital of Saint Augustine.

It seemed like the start of a new era. With California having been settled in the previous decade, and with the unexpected addition of French Louisiana, Spain's empire in what is now the United States stretched for the first time uninterrupted from coast to coast. Spain now governed all the land from the Atlantic beaches of Florida through the Mississippi River Valley and the deserts of the Southwest to the Pacific Coast as far north as San Francisco.

It would not last. Spanish rule in Louisiana ended in 1802 when French leader Napoleon Bonaparte insisted that Spain's weak king, Carlos IV, return the territory to France. Just one year later, Napoleon would sell it to a then-young republic, the United States. With the Louisiana Purchase, the United States vastly expanded its territory.

Florida, too, was heading in a similar direction. After it came under Spanish control for a second time, frictions developed between Spanish colonists and neighboring citizens of the newly independent United States. In 1821 the United States bought Florida from Spain. It was a crucial year—also in 1821, Spain officially recognized the independence of Mexico, which had fought against colonial Spain as Americans had fought for independence from Great Britain. All of the Spanish colonies of the Southwest, from Texas to California, became part of the new nation of Mexico.

The Spanish empire in North America had ended, as Spain no longer governed any territory that today belongs to one of the fifty states. Yet Spain had been in Florida and the Southwest for some 250 years, longer than the United States has been a sovereign country. Its influence can still be felt today, and its heritage can still be seen.

Opposite:
Spain's empire reached from coast to coast after the Treaty of Paris was signed in 1783.

BRITISH NORTH AMERICA

Claimed by
U.S. and
Great
Britain

Claimed by
U.S. and
Great
Britain

Claimed by
NH and NY

L. Superior

L. Michigan

L. Huron

St. Lawrence R.

L. Ontario

L. Erie

Boston

New York

Mississippi R.

Missouri R.

SPANISH

LOUISIANA

NORTHWEST

TERRITORY

(Ceded to U.S. in 1784)

Ohio R.

St. Louis

Claimed by
Virginia

Claimed by
North Carolina

Tennessee R.

Claimed by Georgia

Arkansas R.

Red R.

Santa
Fe

El Paso

Wilmington

Charleston

ATLANTIC
OCEAN

Claimed by Georgia,
Spain, and U.S.

Chattahoochee R.

Natchez

SPANISH FLORIDA

St. Augustine

Pensacola

Rio Grande

New Orleans

*Gulf of
Mexico*

Timeline

1565	Pedro de Avilés founds Saint Augustine, the first permanent European settlement in what is now the United States.
1586	Francis Drake burns down most of Saint Augustine.
1598	Juan de Oñate establishes San Miguel in New Mexico, the first European settlement in the southwest.
1599	A fire and hurricane destroy much of Saint Augustine.
1607	Jamestown, North America's first permanent British colony, is established.
1607	The first Spanish settlement is established on the site of what would become Santa Fe.
1610	Santa Fe is formally founded and named New Mexico's capital.
1620	Pilgrims arrive in Plymouth, Massachusetts.
1630	Friar Alonso de Benavides claims in a published report that 86,000 American Indians have been baptized in New Mexico.
1659	A measles epidemic kills some ten thousand people in Florida.
1670s	Spain's colonies in Florida are at their peak, with some forty missions extending from San Marco on Florida's Gulf Coast to Santa Catalina Island in South Carolina.
1672	Construction of Castillo San Marcos begins in Saint Augustine; the fortress is completed in 1695.
1680	Two thousand Pueblo Indian warriors led by Popé oust Spanish colonists from Santa Fe; on the East Coast, British troops and American Indian allies force Spanish colonists to abandon their northernmost settlements.
1685	The French, under La Salle, establish Fort Louis on the Texas Gulf Coast; it is abandoned by 1689.
1687	Jesuit priest Eusebio Francisco Kino establishes the mission system in southern Arizona.
1693	Diego de Vargas reconquers Santa Fe for Spain.
1698	The Spanish begin construction of a fort at Pensacola.
1702	As part of the War of Spanish Succession in Europe, Governor James Moore of South Carolina attacks Saint Augustine but is forced to withdraw.
1704–1706	Raids by Moore's British troops and American Indian allies destroy most of Spain's forty missions in Florida.

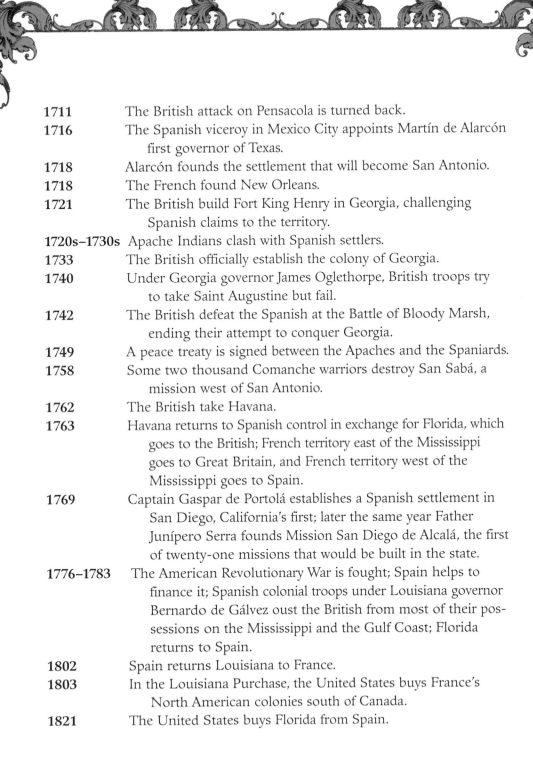

1711	The British attack on Pensacola is turned back.
1716	The Spanish viceroy in Mexico City appoints Martín de Alarcón first governor of Texas.
1718	Alarcón founds the settlement that will become San Antonio.
1718	The French found New Orleans.
1721	The British build Fort King Henry in Georgia, challenging Spanish claims to the territory.
1720s–1730s	Apache Indians clash with Spanish settlers.
1733	The British officially establish the colony of Georgia.
1740	Under Georgia governor James Oglethorpe, British troops try to take Saint Augustine but fail.
1742	The British defeat the Spanish at the Battle of Bloody Marsh, ending their attempt to conquer Georgia.
1749	A peace treaty is signed between the Apaches and the Spaniards.
1758	Some two thousand Comanche warriors destroy San Sabá, a mission west of San Antonio.
1762	The British take Havana.
1763	Havana returns to Spanish control in exchange for Florida, which goes to the British; French territory east of the Mississippi goes to Great Britain, and French territory west of the Mississippi goes to Spain.
1769	Captain Gaspar de Portolá establishes a Spanish settlement in San Diego, California's first; later the same year Father Junípero Serra founds Mission San Diego de Alcalá, the first of twenty-one missions that would be built in the state.
1776–1783	The American Revolutionary War is fought; Spain helps to finance it; Spanish colonial troops under Louisiana governor Bernardo de Gálvez oust the British from most of their possessions on the Mississippi and the Gulf Coast; Florida returns to Spain.
1802	Spain returns Louisiana to France.
1803	In the Louisiana Purchase, the United States buys France's North American colonies south of Canada.
1821	The United States buys Florida from Spain.

Glossary

conquistadores Spanish conquerors of Mexico and Peru in the sixteenth century.

coquina A type of stone consisting of crushed seashells.

criollo A person of European descent born in the Spanish-speaking Americas.

demographics The physical characteristics of a population, such as age, sex, marital status, educaton and geographic location.

dynastic A sequence of rulers from the same family or line.

encomienda A political system used in Spanish colonies in which Indians were forced to work for settlers in exchange for protection and basic schooling in Christianity and Spanish culture.

fanega A measurement of volume used during mission times in California.

floridiano A person of European descent born in colonial Spanish Florida.

feudalism The political system followed in most of Europe during the Middle Ages in which peasants provided military service to the nobility in exchange for protection and a parcel of land in which to plant.

idolatry The worshipping of idols.

mestizos Persons of mixed racial ancestry, especially of mixed European and Native American ancestry.

missions Spanish Catholic settlements led by priests, whose principal duty was to Christianize Indians.

pantheons Groups of gods or other figures of worship of a culture.

peninsulares Settlers in the Spanish Empire who were born in Spain.

presidios Fortresses established in the southwestern United States by the Spanish to protect their holdings and missions.

religious order A group of priests, monks, or nuns with its own vows and regulations.

repartimiento A system used in colonial Spanish America by which Spain allowed certain colonists to recruit Indians for forced labor.

situado A subsidy paid by the Spanish crown to some of the poorer colonies.

tribute A payment made by one person or group to acknowledge the superiority of another and to receive its protection.

unassimilated Not having absorbed the culture of a population or group.

viceroyalty A colonial government that rules as the representative of the king or sovereign.

Further Information

Books

McIntosh, Kenneth. *First Encounters Between Spain and the Americas: Two Worlds Meet* (Hispanic Heritage). Broomall, PA: Mason Crest, 2005.

Stein, R. Conrad. *The Conquistadors: Building a Spanish Empire in the Americas* (Proud Heritage). Mankato, MN: Child's World, 2004.

Wulffson, Don. *Before Columbus: Early Voyages to the Americas*. Brookfield, CT: Twenty-First Century Books, 2007.

Zinn, Howard, and Stefoff, Rebecca. *A Young People's History of the United States: Columbus to the Spanish-American War*. New York: Seven Stories Press, 2007.

Web Sites

General History of Spain in the United States

http://www.latinamericanstudies.org

> One of the Web's largest collections of information about the Hispanic world; includes links about the Spanish Empire in the United States.

http://international.loc.gov/intldl/eshtml/eshome.html

> This Library of Congress site explores Spain and the United States in America from the fifteenth to the nineteenth centuries.

Spanish California

http://missionsofcalifornia.org

> Home page of the California Missions Foundation.

Spanish Florida

http://www.nps.gov/casa

> Home page of Castillo de San Marcos National Monument.

http://www.historicstaugustine.com

> St. Augustine's Colonial Spanish Quarter "living museum."

The Spanish Southwest

http://www.nps.gov/saan

> Home page of San Antonio Missions National Historical Park.

http://nmtourism.org/go/loc/favorites/page/attractions-missions.html

> The official New Mexico tourist guide to the state's Spanish missions.

http://www.nps.gov/archive/tuma/Kino_Missions.html

> A look at Arizona's mission system from the National Park Service.

Bibliography

Henderson, Ann L. and Mormino, Gary R., editors. *Spanish Pathways in Florida*. Sarasota, FL: Pineapple Press, 1991.

Hernández, Roger E., and Anton, Alex. *Cubans in America*. New York: Kensington Books, 2002.

Kessell, John L. *Spain in the Southwest: A Narrative History of Colonial New Mexico, Arizona, Texas, and California*. Norman: University of Oklahoma Press, 2003.

Manucy, Albert. *Sixteenth Century St. Agustine: The People and Their Homes*. Gainesville: University Press of Florida, 1997.

Weber, David J. *The Spanish Frontier in North America*. New Haven, CT: Yale University Press, 1992.

INDEX

About the Author

ROGER E. HERNÁNDEZ writes a nationally syndicated column distributed by King Features to some forty daily newspapers across the country. He is also Writer in Residence at the New Jersey Institute of Technology and author of *Cubans in America*. Hernández was born in Cuba and came to the United States as a child in 1965, when his parents fled the Castro regime.